MARS

A TRUE BOOK

by

Larry Dane Brimner

Children's Press®
A Division of Grolier Publishing

New York London Hong Kong Sydney
Danbury, Connecticut

A Martian meteorite may hold the secret to life on Mars.

Subject Consultant
Peter Goodwin
Science Department Chairman
Kent School, Kent, CT

Reading Consultant
Linda Cornwell
Learning Resource Consultant
Indiana Department
of Education

Author's Dedication:
For Colony Bend
Elementary School

Visit Children's Press® on the Internet at:
http://publishing.grolier.com

Library of Congress Cataloging-in-Publication Data

Brimner, Larry Dane.
   Mars / by Larry Dane Brimner.
     p.   cm. — (A true book)
   Includes bibliographical references and index.
   Summary: Simple facts about the Red Planet such as its orbit, atmosphere, and terrain, as well as the outcomes of explorations such as the Pathfinder Mission.
   ISBN 0-516-20618-4 (lib. bdg.)   0-516-26435-4 (pbk.)
   1. Mars (Planet)—Exploration—Juvenile literature. 2. Astronautics in astronomy—Juvenile literature. [1. Mars (Planet)—Exploration. 2. Space flight to Mars.] I. Title. II. Series.
QB641.B75 1998
523.43—dc21

                91-42072
                CIP
                AC

Contents

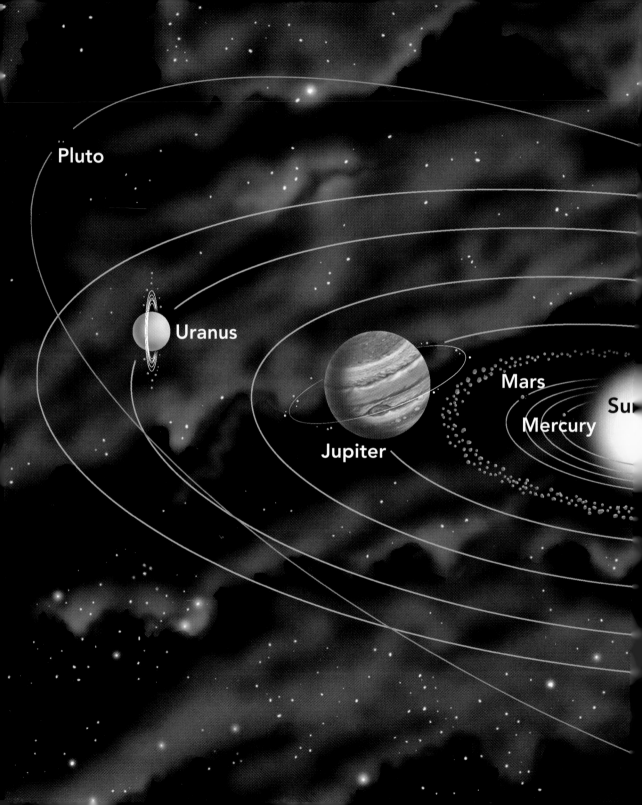

The Solar System

Venus

Earth

Moon

Asteroid Belt

Saturn

Neptune

The Red Planet

Mars has always been a planet of mystery. To observers on Earth, it looks like a red disk. Its color comes from the red dust on its surface. When the red dust gets stirred up by strong winds, the planet's red color is even more intense. This explains why Mars, the fourth

Mars can be seen
clearly in the night sky.

planet from the Sun, is some-
times called the Red Planet.

Long ago, however, people
thought the reddish color
came from blood. Because
wars cause bloodshed, they

MARS.

Mars was the Roman god of war. The symbol for Mars (above) looks like a shield and spear.

named the planet Mars—after the Roman god of war. Even the ancient symbol for Mars, a circle with an arrow, represents a shield and spear. Such a fierce image led people to think wild things about Earth's neighbor in the solar system.

Old Ideas

When early astronomers first looked through their telescopes, they saw similarities between Earth and Mars. By 1659, Christiaan Huygens, a Dutch astronomer, had discovered that Mars rotates, or spins, as it orbits, or travels, around the Sun. He measured

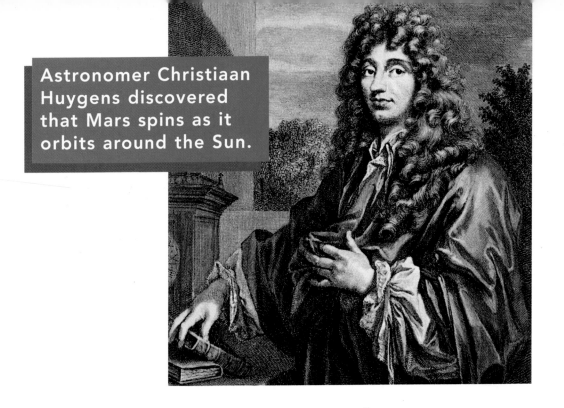

the time it took for Mars to make one complete rotation— or one Mars "day." It was nearly the same as Earth's rotation. Today we know that Mars's "day" is equal to 24 hours and 37.5 minutes.

By the end of the 1700s, astronomer William Herschel had seen ice caps at both of Mars's poles. He knew that Mars tilts on its axis much as

Ice caps can be seen at both the north and south poles of Mars.

Herschel thought the dark spots he saw on Mars were oceans. Today, we know they are volcanoes.

Earth does. Since Earth's tilt creates the seasons as it orbits the Sun, it made sense to Herschel that Mars must also have seasons. He also saw dark spots on the planet's surface, which he thought were oceans. Based on these findings, Herschel decided that Martians probably lived in a world much like our own Earth.

In 1877, astronomer Giovanni Schiaparelli made a startling finding. When he looked through his telescope, he saw long, straight lines on the Martian surface. He called them *canali*, which means either "channels" or "canals" in Italian. Canals? If there were

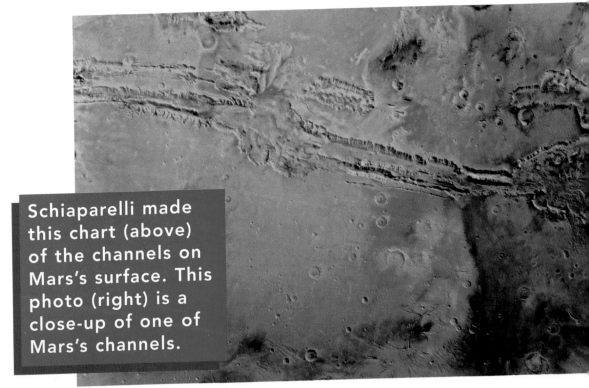

Schiaparelli made this chart (above) of the channels on Mars's surface. This photo (right) is a close-up of one of Mars's channels.

canals, or waterways, there had to be Martians to build them. American astronomer Percival Lowell guessed that the canals were used to move water from the Martian ice caps to the deserts. This meant that Martians must be very intelligent—maybe more intelligent than humans.

While Schiaparelli and Lowell were observing Martian "canals," Asaph Hall was discovering Mars's two moons.

Phobos, the larger of Mars's two moons

He named them *Phobos* and *Deimos*, words that mean "fear" and "panic" in the Greek language.

For a while, many people believed that super-intelligent beings lived on Mars. They also still connected Mars to the idea of war. Many people assumed that if there were Martians, they must be unfriendly.

This set the stage for the most famous radio show in history. It was broadcast in 1938 and was called *The War of the Worlds*. The show began with music, which was soon interrupted. A news flash announced that New Jersey was being invaded by Martians!

The radio show *The War of the Worlds* scared people into thinking that New Jersey had been invaded by Martians.

It was only a radio show, a play, but it set off a real panic. People ran from their homes. They crowded onto roadways to escape the Martian invasion—an invasion that wasn't happening anywhere except on the radio.

A Closer Look

By observing the Red Planet, astronomers learned much about it. They learned that it travels on an elliptical path, like a stretched-out circle, as it orbits the Sun. They also discovered that Herschel was correct when he thought that Mars had seasons. Its seasons,

From the way Mars is tilted, astronomer William Herschel correctly assumed that Mars has seasons.

however, are twice as long as those on Earth because it takes Mars—which is only half the size of Earth—687 Earth-days to orbit the Sun. This is almost twice as long as Earth's 365-day journey around the Sun.

Most of what we know about Mars has been learned since astronomers sent *Mariner 4* to take a closer look. Launched on November 28, 1964, *Mariner 4* came within 6,080 miles (9,790 kilometers) of Mars in mid-July 1965. It sent back twenty-two pictures of the Martian surface. The pictures showed no Martian cities, only a world with many craters, just like our Moon. Mars appeared to be a lifeless, red desert.

Mars's cratered surface looks a lot like Earth's Moon.

Mariner 4 also revealed that Mars's atmosphere (the gases that surround Mars) is very thin. It is mostly made up of carbon dioxide, one of the gases that we breathe out of our bodies.

When *Mariner 9* went into orbit around Mars in 1971, the pictures it took showed even more interesting details. When *Mariner 9* began to take its pictures, a dust storm was raging. Nothing could be seen except some peaks that rose above the blowing dust. Later, it became clear that the peaks were actually four large volcanoes. One of them, Olympus Mons, is thought to be the largest volcano in the solar system. Its peak soars 15 miles

Olympus Mons may be the largest volcano in the solar system.

(24 km) above the surrounding surface—almost three times the height of Mount Everest, Earth's highest peak.

Mariner 9 also revealed something else that scientists found exciting—channels.

These were not the *canali* that Schiaparelli and Lowell thought they saw. These were river channels, now dry. If there had been water on Mars, could there also have been life?

The channels on Mars's surface were carved by rivers long ago.

Searching for Life

In 1976, two *Viking* spacecraft landed on Mars to find out if there was life on the Red Planet. The *Viking* landers were like small science laboratories. They had scoops to collect Martian soil, cameras to take pictures, and instruments to run tests. The experiments, however,

This model of the *Viking 2* lander shows its tilted position as it landed on Mars.

proved very little about Mars—except that there were no signs of life.

The last information received from the *Viking* landers was sent to Earth in November

1982. The people at the National Aeronautics and Space Administration (NASA) remained curious, though. Could the *Viking* landers have missed something? After all, the soil samples they tested were very small. There may be no life on Mars now, but could there have been life in the past?

Most scientists today believe that Mars is a lifeless planet. Some scientists, however, think

The Face

In 1976, *Viking 1* photographed this incredible image on the Martian surface. Scientists believe this image of a "human face" was made by shadows cast on mountains and cliffs. Some people believe the features were "designed" as a message from alien beings. What do you think? Starting in 1998, the *Mars Global Surveyor* will orbit the planet and re-photograph "The Face." NASA hopes to prove which belief is correct.

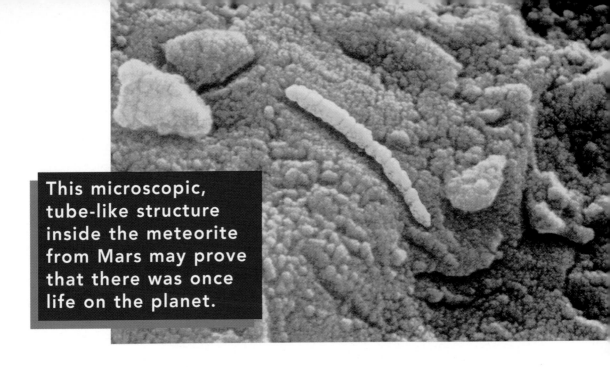

This microscopic, tube-like structure inside the meteorite from Mars may prove that there was once life on the planet.

that life of some kind may have existed there in the past. No one knows for sure. In August 1996, scientists studied a Martian meteorite, or rock fragment, found in Antarctica. They said it may hold the remains of a living thing from long ago.

Mars Pathfinder

NASA launched *Mars Pathfinder* on December 4, 1996, to search for more answers. It reached Mars on July 4, 1997, bouncing for 92 seconds across the Martian surface on airbags before coming to a stop. The airbags protected *Pathfinder* and the robot

Pathfinder held the six-wheeled robot *Sojourner* inside.

named *Sojourner*, which means "traveler," that it held inside.

Once *Pathfinder*, also called "the Sagan lander" after the late astronomer Carl Sagan, came to a rest, its panels opened. A scientist on Earth used a computer to send instructions to *Pathfinder*. *Sojourner*, looking like a six-wheeled

This scientist "drove" *Sojourner* across Mars from his computer on Earth.

skateboard, rolled down a ramp and onto the Martian surface to begin its work.

Progress was slow. *Sojourner* moved less than .5 inches (1.3 centimeters) per second. This slow pace kept *Sojourner* from running into trouble before scientists on Earth could send it directions.

Almost immediately, NASA scientists began to receive information. *Sojourner* used its cameras, weather-sensing

Once down *Pathfinder's* ramp, *Sojourner* set out to explore a nearby rock.

equipment, and spectrometer—an instrument that tells scientists what rocks and soil are made of—to collect information. Designed to last thirty *sols*, or Martian days, the robot lasted even longer.

Scientists chose Ares Vallis as *Pathfinder*'s landing site because they believed it would have rock samples from all over Mars.

Sojourner was the first robot to explore another planet.
Scientists chose *Pathfinder*'s landing site, an area called Ares Vallis, because it could

give them a lot of information about the planet. Ares Vallis is a dusty lowland today, but it was once flooded by rivers. These rivers had carried rocks from all parts of Mars. So *Sojourner* was able to sample rocks from many different parts of Mars without traveling too far. Some of the information from *Sojourner* may tell us whether conditions were ever right to support life on Mars.

Mars Quick Facts

Diameter	4,219 miles (6,790 km)
Average distance from the Sun	142 million miles (230 million km)
Surface temperature	–10°F to –150°F (–23°C to –101°C) *(Sojourner found that temperatures can change 20 degrees in one second.)*
Length of day	24 hours and 37.5 minutes
Length of year	687 Earth-days
Moons	2

Some Missions to Mars

Mission	Launch Date
Mariner 4 (USA)	November 1964
Mariner 6 (USA)	February 1969
Mariner 7 (USA)	March 1969
Mariner 9 (USA)	May 1971
Mars 2 (USSR)	May 1971
Mars 3 (USSR)	May 1971
Viking 1 (USA)	August 1975
Viking 2 (USA)	September 1975
Mars Global Surveyor (USA)	November 1996
Mars Pathfinder (USA)	December 1996

What's Ahead?

Scientists have not finished exploring Mars. *Mars Global Surveyor*, launched before *Pathfinder* in 1996, will photograph and map the planet's surface. It will not land on the planet like *Pathfinder* did. Instead, it will orbit the planet for over two years and

Workers prepare the *Mars Global Surveyor* spacecraft for launch.

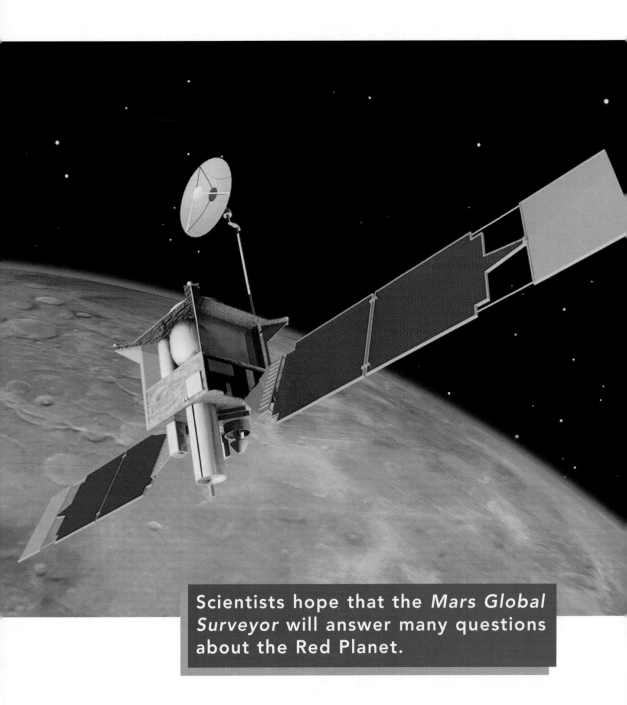

Scientists hope that the *Mars Global Surveyor* will answer many questions about the Red Planet.

collect information. By 2005 Martian landers will start bringing pieces of Mars back to Earth. The scientists who study the pieces may find the answers to our questions about life on Mars.

Eventually, astronauts may join the exploration team. Even then, Mars will remain what it has always been—a mystery. There will always be something new to discover about the Red Planet.

To Find Out More

Here are more places to learn about Mars and other planets in space:

 **Books**

Asimov, Isaac. **Mars: Our Mysterious Neighbor.** Gareth Stevens Publishing, 1988.

Asimov, Isaac. **The Red Planet: Mars.** Gareth Stevens Publishing, 1994.

Brewer, Duncan. **Mars.** Marshall Cavendish Corporation, 1993.

Getz, David. **Life on Mars.** Henry Holt & Co., 1997.

Landau, Elaine. **Mars.** Franklin Watts, 1996.

Organizations and Online Sites

The Children's Museum of Indianapolis

3000 N. Meridian Street
Indianapolis, IN 46208-4716
(317) 924-5431
http://childrensmuseum. org/sq1.htm

Visit the SpaceQuest Planetarium to see what it has to offer, including a view of this month's night sky.

National Aeronautics and Space Administration (NASA)

http://www.nasa.gov

At NASA's home page, you can access information about its exciting history and present resources and missions.

National Air and Space Museum

Smithsonian Institution
601 Independence Ave. SW
Washington, DC 20560
(202) 357-1300
http://www.nasm.si.edu/

The National Air and Space Museum site gives you up-to-date information about its programs and exhibits.

The Nine Planets

http://seds.lpl.arizona.edu/ nineplanets/nineplanets/

Take a multimedia tour of the solar system and all its planets and moons.

Space Telescope Science Institute

3700 San Martin Drive
Johns Hopkins University
Homewood Campus
Baltimore, MD 21218
(410) 338-4700
http://www.stsci.edu//

The Space Telescope Science Institute operates the Hubble Space Telescope. Visit this site to see pictures of the telescope's outer-space view.

Windows to the Universe

http://windows.engin. umich.edu/

This site lets you click on all nine planets to find information about each one. It also covers many other space subjects, including important historical figures, scientists, and astronauts.

Important Words

astronomer a scientist who studies objects in space

atmosphere the gases that surround a planet

axis an imaginary line about which a planet turns

canals waterways

elliptical shaped like a stretched-out circle

ice caps large areas of ice

meteorite a fragment, or piece, of rock

orbit to travel around an object

pole either end of a planet's axis

rotate to spin

spectrometer an instrument that tells scientists what rocks and soil are made of

telescope an instrument that makes far-away objects look closer

Index

WAHON

Meet the Author

Larry Dane Brimner is the author of more than fifty books for young readers. His many other titles in the True Book series include: *E-mail, The World Wide Web,* and *The Winter Olympics.* He travels often to speak to elementary school students about the writing process, but he has never been to Mars.

Photographs ©: AP/Wide World Photos: 18; Corbis-Bettmann: 32, 33 (Agence France Presse), 8, 14 top; Greg Harris: 4-5; NASA: 11, 12, 22, 24, 35, 41; Photo Researchers: 42 (Julian Baum), 1, 2, 29, 30, 36 (NASA/SPL), 7 (Rev. Ronald Royer), 16, 39 right (SPL), cover, 14 bottom, 25, 38, 39 left (U.S. Geological Survey/SPL); Photri: 27; Superstock, Inc.: 10 (Stock Montage); The Mary Lea Shane Archives of the Lick Observatory, The University Library, University of California: 20.